MISS PEACH

was launched on February 4, 1957, "the day my life changed," says Mell Lazarus, and the more fruitful half of his career was under way.

Mell has been writing and drawing MISS PEACH ever since. MISS PEACH is a young schoolteacher who contends with a classroom of rather sophisticated kids named Arthur and Marcia and Ira and a world full of politics, reading, writing, arithmetic and the general silliness of contemporary society. Mell's grasp of the absurdities of modern life is surpassed only by that of the tiny people in his comic strip.

Since October, 1970, Mell has also been writing MOMMA. The fact that he has two popular strips in national syndication he regards as "a very small distinction in life, probably reflecting a certain amount of greed and masochism."

He has also written a novel (THE BOSS IS CRAZY, TOO) and three off-Broadway plays (EVERY-BODY INTO THE LAKE, ELLIMAN AND THE FLY, LIFETIME OF EGGCREAMS).

Mell is a native of New York City who lives in Los Angeles and Palm Springs, California. He has three daughters, the youngest of whom, Catherine, lives with him. Marjorie and Susan, married and engaged, respectively, live nearby and are very much involved in his life. So is Momma.

IT'S LONELY
AT THE TOP

MELL LAZARUS

BANTAM BOOKS
Toronto / New York / London / Sydney

IT'S LONELY AT THE TOP
A Bantam Book / November 1981

ISBN 0-553-20037-2

Published simultaneously in the United States and Canada

Bantam Books are published by Bantam Books, Inc. Its trademark, consisting of the words "Bantam Books" and the por-
trayal of a rooster, is Registered in U.S. Patent and Trademark
Office and in other countries. Marca Registrada. Bantam
Books, Inc., 666 Fifth Avenue, New York, New York 10103.

PRINTED IN THE UNITED STATES OF AMERICA

0 9 8 7 6 5 4 3 2 1

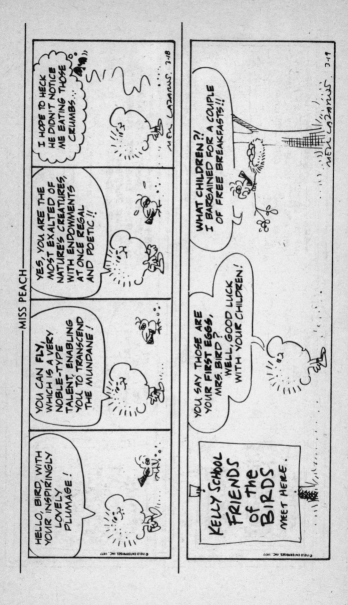

MISS PEACH

ARTHUR POINTS OUT CHEERING HARBINGERS OF SPRING
ARTHUR, TELL ME A SIGN OF SPRING!
HERE'S ONE: YESTERDAY, USING A METAL DETECTOR, MY FATHER FINALLY WAS ABLE TO LOCATE OUR CAR UNDER THE SNOW IN OUR DRIVEWAY....
MELL LAZARUS. 3-21
© FIELD ENTERPRISES, INC., 1977

ARTHUR POINTS OUT Encouraging SIGNS of SPRING
ARTHUR, TELL ME A SIGN OF SPRING!
HERE'S ONE: THIS MORNING I NOTICED MILLIONS OF ANTS, IN A LONG, BLACK LINE, STREAMING INTO OUR GARDEN, FROM OUR KITCHEN...
MELL LAZARUS. 3-22
© FIELD ENTERPRISES, INC., 1977

MISS PEACH

EVERYONE HAS A PHILOSOPHY OF LIFE. IRA, WOULD YOU CARE TO TELL US YOURS?
ARE YOU FAMILIAR WITH THE WORKS OF FEODOR DOSTOEVSKY, MISS PEACH?
WHY, YES!
WELL, WHAT HE SAID GOES FOR ME, TOO.
4-1
MELL LAZARUS.
© FIELD ENTERPRISES, INC., 1977

ARTHUR, WHY DON'T YOU LEARN TO THINK?
EVERYONE THINKS, PLANS, FIGURES THINGS OUT, TO MAKE THEIR LIVES EASIER AND MORE PRODUCTIVE. WHY NOT **YOU**?
I LIKE TO THINK OF STUPIDITY AS ONE OF THOSE "ALTERNATIVE LIFE-STYLES."
4-2
MELL LAZARUS.
© FIELD ENTERPRISES, INC., 1977

ARTHUR, I WANT YOU TO RAISE YOUR SCHOLASTIC STANDING BY USING THE NATIVE INTELLIGENCE WE ALL KNOW YOU HAVE!
PRINCIPAL
I'LL TRY, MR. GRIMMIS – BUT DON'T EXPECT MY USE OF MY INTELLIGENCE TO SHOW UP IN ANY FANCY DISPLAY OF BRAINS...
MELL LAZARUS. 4-4
© FIELD ENTERPRISES, INC., 1977

CHILDREN, TODAY WE'RE GOING TO FINGER-PAINT, WHICH IS THE GREATEST, MOST EXCITING THING EVER!
GEE. I HOPE THE REST OF OUR LIVES AREN'T JUST ONE LONG ANTI-CLIMAX...
MELL LAZARUS. 4-5
© FIELD ENTERPRISES, INC., 1977

MISS PEACH

WALTER, YOU KNOW HOW THE FIRST AUTOMOBILE CAME TO BE BUILT?
BY THE INVENTOR, IN HIS BACKYARD, OUT OF PIECES OF SCRAP METAL AND STUFF.
RIGHT! AND WHEN IT WAS FINISHED, I GUESS HE BORROWED THE KEYS FROM HIS FATHER...
MELL LAZARUS. 4-8
© FIELD ENTERPRISES, INC., 1977

ARTHUR WANTS TO BE A MILLIONAIRE WHEN HE GROWS UP?
YES, MISS PEACH, BUT HE THINKS HE CAN DO IT WITHOUT RESOURCES!
ARTHUR, TO BE A MILLIONAIRE, YOU NEED MONEY, AND STOCKS, BONDS, SECURITIES, AND SO FORTH!
NONSENSE! A **REAL** MILLIONAIRE DOESN'T NEED PROPS...
MELL LAZARUS
4-9
© FIELD ENTERPRISES, INC. 1977

MISS PEACH

MR. GRIMMIS, WE THINK YOU ARE POMPOUS, OFFICIOUS, AND TRYING TO RUN EVERYONE'S LIFE!
ISN'T THAT A BIT PRESUMPTUOUS?
PRINCIPAL
YES, AND THAT'S WHY WE'RE SO MAD ABOUT IT!
4-11
MELL LAZARUS.
© FIELD ENTERPRISES, INC. 1977

KELLY SCHOOL STUDENT COURT
MARCIA PRESIDING →
IRA, BAILIFF
YOUR HONOR, EVERYONE HAS BEEN BEHAVING LATELY, SO THERE ARE NO CASES TO TRY! WHY DON'T WE PACK IT IN AND SPLIT THE SCENE?
YOU'RE UNDER ARREST FOR USING SLANG TO A JUDGE.
MELL LAZARUS.
4-12
© FIELD ENTERPRISES, INC. 1977

MISS PEACH

FUTURE DOCTORS of AMERICA MEET HERE →
ARTHUR, YOU SAY MEDICAL SCIENCE, EVEN THE PRESENT ADVANCED STATE OF THE ART, STILL IS NOT PERFECT? CAN YOU GIVE ME AN EXAMPLE?
JUST LAST WEEK I READ A PAPER IN THE A.M.A. JOURNAL ABOUT AN OFFICE COMPUTER THAT FORGOT TO SEND OUT A BILL ...
MELL LAZARUS. 4-13
© FIELD ENTERPRISES, INC., 1977

AH! CAN I ASSUME YOU HAVE PLANTED VEGETABLES?
KELLY SCHOOL KINDERGARTEN GARDEN
NO. OVER THERE ARE MINERALS AND THIS PART IS ANIMALS...
4-14 MELL LAZARUS.
© FIELD ENTERPRISES, INC., 1977

MISS PEACH

MARCIA'S ADVICE FOR BOYS with PROBLEMS with GIRLS
WHEN A GIRL TELLS A BOY SHE LOVES HIM, HOW CAN HE BE SURE SHE MEANS IT?
IN YOUR CASE, HAVE HER HEAD EXAMINED.
4-15

SEE THIS FIST, IRA? IT'S MY SECRET WEAPON. WITH IT, I CAN PUNCH ANYBODY OUT. THEREFORE, NOBODY EVER PUSHES ME AROUND!!
DO YOU FREE-LANCE?
4-16

MISS PEACH

IRA, YOU SAY YOU FEEL PUT DOWN ALL THE TIME, EXCEPT FOR OCCASIONAL MOMENTS OF EXALTATION? WHEN **ARE** THOSE MOMENTS?
SCHOOL PSYCHOLOGIST
WHEN SOMEBODY INVENTS A NEW, FRESH, SPARKLINGLY ORIGINAL EPITHET JUST FOR ME!
MELL LAZARUS.
4-18
© FIELD ENTERPRISES, INC., 1977

KELLY SCHOOL KLARION NEWS ROOM →
ARTHUR, HOW LONG IS THAT CAREFULLY INCISIVE, IN-DEPTH REVIEW OF THE SCHOOL PLAY YOU'VE WRITTEN?
EDITOR
CITY
DRAMA
I'M AFRAID IT'S ONLY 5,000 WORDS, CHIEF. IT WOULD HAVE BEEN LONGER IF I'D HAD A CHANCE TO **SEE** THE PLAY...
MELL LAZARUS.
4-19
© FIELD ENTERPRISES, INC., 1977

MISS PEACH

KELLY SCHOOL KLARION
NEWS ROOM
ARTHUR, DO YOU HAVE A HEADLINE FOR THAT STORY ABOUT IRA DONATING A GORGEOUS NEW TEST-TUBE TO THE SCHOOL, AND THE CHEM TEACHER APPRECIATING IT SO MUCH, SHE LIFTED IRA CLEAR OFF THE FLOOR AND HUGGED HIM?
EDITOR
SPORTS
YES, CHIEF: "SNAPPY RETORT TO AUTHORITIES CAUSES IRA'S SUSPENSION."
EDUCATION
MELL LAZARUS.
4-20

KELLY SCHOOL KLARION
EDITORIAL OFFICES →
ARTHUR, WHAT'S THE HEADLINE FOR THE STORY ABOUT THE POTTED GERANIUM THAT GOT KNOCKED OFF THE DESK BY LINDA'S ELBOW, CAUSING A COLONY OF APHIDS TO STOP CHEWING ON THE LEAVES?
EDITOR
CITY
"PLANT STRUCK; THOUSANDS OUT OF WORK."
GARDEN
MELL LAZARUS.
4-21

MISS PEACH

KELLY SCHOOL KLARION
NEWS ROOM →
ARTHUR, WE NEED A HEADLINE ON YOUR STORY ABOUT MR. GRIMMIS JOGGING FIVE MILES TO SCHOOL WITHOUT EVEN BREATHING HARD, AND CLAIMING HE WAS ABLE TO DO IT BECAUSE HE PUT THE THOUGHT OF FATIGUE COMPLETELY OUT OF HIS MIND.
EDITOR
SPORTS
HOW ABOUT, "PRINCIPAL COMES TO SCHOOL WITHOUT PANTS; SAY IT WAS DUE TO POOR MEMORY."
MELL LAZARUS.
4-22
© FIELD ENTERPRISES, INC., 1977

IRA, YOU SAY YOU SOMETIMES FEEL UNDISTINGUISHED? EVERYONE FEELS THAT WAY ONE TIME OR ANOTHER!
THANKS A LOT!!
MELL LAZARUS.
4-23
© FIELD ENTERPRISES, INC., 1977

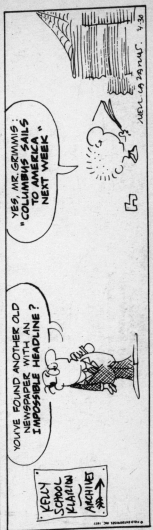

MISS PEACH

IRA GIVES ADVICE ON GOOD TASTE
LAST SUNDAY I REFUSED TO KISS MY AUNT, EVEN AFTER SHE GAVE ME $5.00 FOR MY BIRTHDAY. DID I COMMIT A FAUX PAS?
YES, A SERIOUS ONE. HOWEVER, YOU CAN REMEDY IT BY COMING OVER TO MY HOUSE NEXT SUNDAY AND KISSING MY AUNT.
MELL LAZARUS. 5-2
© FIELD ENTERPRISES, INC., 1977

KELLY SCHOOL KLARION ARCHIVES
YOU HAVE AN IMPOSSIBLE BIRTH ANNOUNCEMENT FROM AN OLD NEWSPAPER, ARTHUR?
YES, I DO: "ITHACA, N.Y., AUG. 11, 1921 — ALEX HALEY, GREAT-GREAT-GREAT-GREAT-GREAT GRANDSON OF KUNTA KINTE, BORN TODAY."
1920
1921
MELL LAZARUS. 5-3
© FIELD ENTERPRISES, INC., 1977

MISS PEACH

MISS PEACH

MISS PEACH

IRA, I SENT FOR YOU ON MONDAY, AND HERE YOU ARE, SHOWING UP ON FRIDAY!!
PRINCIPAL
RIGHT, MR. GRIMMIS. UNTIL NOW, I COULDN'T THINK OF A PLAUSIBLE EXCUSE FOR NOT SHOWING UP ON MONDAY...!
MEL LAZARUS.
5-13
© FIELD ENTERPRISES, INC., 1977

LINDA, YOU PUNCHED IRA. I'LL HAVE TO FIND AGAINST YOU, UNLESS THERE WERE VERY GOOD REASONS FOR WHAT YOU DID!
KELLY SCHOOL STUDENT COURT
OH, THERE WERE, YOUR HONOR! I FELT LIKE PUNCHING SOMEONE, AND IRA'S FACE IS SO PUNCHABLE!
CASE DISMISSED.
MEL LAZARUS. 5-14
© FIELD ENTERPRISES, INC., 1977

YOU WANT TO STOP COMING HERE, IRA? WELL, I'M AFRAID I CAN'T GIVE YOU A CLEAN BILL OF HEALTH!
SCHOOL PSYCHOLOGIST
HOW ABOUT A SLIGHTLY SOILED BILL OF HEALTH?
5-16
MELL LAZARUS.
© FIELD ENTERPRISES, INC., 1977

ARTHUR'S SUMMER VACATION ADVICE
I'M HARD PUT TO DECIDE BETWEEN TWO WEEKS AT KAMP KELLY, OR A LAVISH PACIFIC CRUISE ON MY RICH UNCLE'S SEA-GOING YACHT....
IF YOU'RE REALLY THAT HARD PUT, I'D SUGGEST THE COUNTY SANITARIUM....
MELL LAZARUS.
5-17
© FIELD ENTERPRISES, INC., 1977

MISS PEACH

—MISS PEACH—

MISS PEACH

IRA, YOU MUST NOT REGARD YOUR HOME AS A PLACE OF STRICT RULES AND REGULATIONS, NOR YOUR PARENTS AS FIGURES OF OPPRESSION ...
SCHOOL PSYCHOLOGIST
OKAY, SO HOW COME EVERY NIGHT THEY TAKE AWAY MY BELT, NECKTIE AND SHOELACES ?
MELL LAZARUS
5-30
© FIELD ENTERPRISES, INC., 1977

NOW THEY'VE BEGUN WATER RATIONING IN CALIFORNIA ....
YES, AND NATURAL GAS WILL SOON BE RATIONED AS WELL, MISS PEACH.
MAYBE WE AMERICANS SIMPLY CONSUME TOO MUCH?
RIGHT! THEY SAY IF WE OWNED THE SAHARA DESERT, IN TWO WEEKS THERE'D BE A SHORTAGE OF SAND ...
MELL LAZARUS,
5-31
© FIELD ENTERPRISES, INC., 1977

MISS PEACH

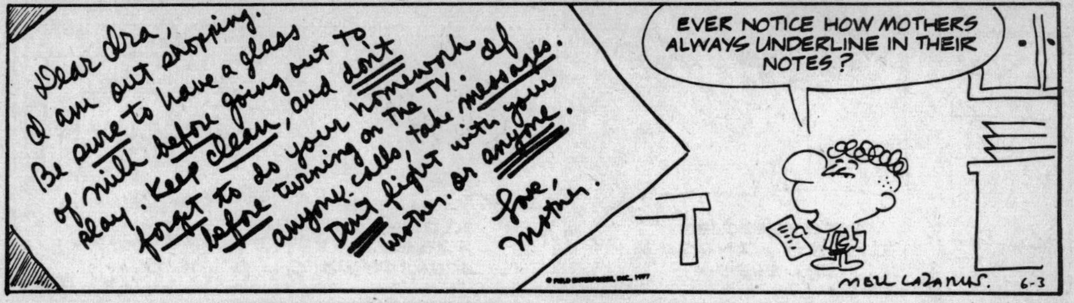
Dear Ira,
I am out shopping.
Be sure to have a glass of milk before going out to play. Keep clean, and don't forget to do your homework before turning on the TV. If anyone calls, take messages. Don't fight with your brother, or anyone.
Love, Mother.
EVER NOTICE HOW MOTHERS ALWAYS UNDERLINE IN THEIR NOTES?
© FIELD ENTERPRISES, INC. 1977
MELL LAZARUS.
6-3

DON'T WORRY, IRA, A PERSON ISN'T DISLIKED JUST BECAUSE HE'S AFRAID OF CERTAIN THINGS.
NOR, ON THE OTHER HAND, IS A PERSON BETTER-LIKED SIMPLY BECAUSE HE HAS NO FEARS..!
-AND THAT'S ANOTHER THING I'M AFRAID OF.!!
© FIELD ENTERPRISES, INC. 1977
MELL LAZARUS.
6-4

MISS PEACH

ARTHUR'S ADVICE ON HOW TO LIVE A HAPPY LIFE
ISN'T IT TRUE THAT ONLY A **HAPPY** PERSON CAN MAKE ANOTHER PERSON HAPPY?
YES, UNLESS THE HAPPY PERSON GOT THAT WAY ON MONEY HE BORROWED FROM THAT OTHER PERSON.
MELL LAZARUS.
6-8
© FIELD ENTERPRISES, INC., 1977

ARTHUR'S ADVICE ON HOW TO LIVE A HAPPIER LIFE
CAN MONEY BRING YOU HAPPINESS?
NO, BUT IT CAN BUY OFF A LOT OF MISERY....
MELL LAZARUS.
6-9
© FIELD ENTERPRISES INC. 1977

MISS PEACH

ARTHUR'S ADVICE ON HOW TO LIVE A HAPPY LIFE
WHERE IS IT WRITTEN THAT WE'RE SUPPOSED TO BE HAPPY?
WHAT DO YOU MEAN !?! IT'S CARVED ON MY DESK IN OUR HOME ROOM!!
MELL LAZARUS.
6-10
© FIELD ENTERPRISES, INC. 1977

ARTHUR'S ADVICE ON HOW TO LIVE A HAPPY LIFE
HOW CAN I BE HAPPY IN LIFE?
STOP WASTING IT BY ASKING FOOLISH QUESTIONS.
MELL LAZARUS.
6-11
© FIELD ENTERPRISES, INC. 1977

MISS PEACH

KELLY KLARION ARCHIVES
HISTORICAL HEADLINES DEP'T.
WHAT WAS THE HEADLINE THE DAY A TRANSPORTER OF NIGHT-STICKS WAS A GUEST IN WASHINGTON?
"BILLY CARTER STAYS AT WHITE HOUSE."
MELL LAZARUS
6-17
© FIELD ENTERPRISES, INC., 1977

KELLY KLARION ARCHIVES
HISTORICAL HEADLINES DEPT.
ARTHUR, WHAT WAS THE HEADLINE THE DAY THAT FAMOUS SONGWRITER FINALLY BECAME IMPRESSED BY THAT NEW YORK BASEBALL TEAM?
"YANKS REACH BERLIN."
MELL LAZARUS
6-18
© FIELD ENTERPRISES, INC., 1977

MISS PEACH

ARTHUR'S FREE MEDICAL ADVICE
I'VE GOT A PAIN IN THE NECK.
TELL HIM, NOT ME.
MELL LAZARUS 6-22
© FIELD ENTERPRISES, INC., 1977

IRA, THE ONLY PEOPLE YOU HAVE TO FEAR ARE THOSE WHO ARE AFRAID OF YOU!
SCHOOL PSYCHOLOGIST
I'M AFRAID THERE'S NOBODY IN THAT CATEGORY...
MELL LAZARUS 6-23
© FIELD ENTERPRISES, INC., 1977

MISS PEACH

WELCOME TO KAMP KELLY
NOW LISTEN UP AND LISTEN GOOD: KEEP THEM BUNKS CLEAN, WASH THEM SOCKS, AND OBEY THEM RULES...
I LOVE IT: PUT DIRT UNDER MR. GRIMMIS' FEET, AND HE TURNS INTO JOHN WAYNE ...
6-27
MEL LAZARUS.
© FIELD ENTERPRISES, INC., 1977

IRA, LAST YEAR HERE AT CAMP, YOU HAD TROUBLE WITH YOUR PEER-GROUP. NOW THAT YOU'RE OLDER, WILL YOU HAVE LESS TROUBLE?
CAMP PSYCHOLOGIST
ONLY IF EVERYONE ELSE HAS STAYED THE SAME AGE...
MEL LAZARUS. 6-28
© FIELD ENTERPRISES, INC., 1977

MISS PEACH

FUTURE LAWYERS of AMERICA MEET HERE →
CHIEF JUSTICE BURGER SAYS NON-LAWYERS COULD HELP SETTLE MANY DISPUTES CHEAPER AND FASTER THAN LAWYERS. WOULDN'T THAT HURT OUR BUSINESS?
NO. THEY'LL STILL NEED US LAWYERS TO START THE DISPUTES.
MELL LAZARUS. 6-29
© FIELD ENTERPRISES, INC., 1977

FUTURE LAWYERS of AMERICA MEET HERE →
IF THERE ARE MORE LAWYERS IN THE U.S., PER CAPITA, THAN ANY OTHER COUNTRY IN THE WORLD, WILL THERE BE ENOUGH LAWSUITS FOR ALL OF US?
NOT TO WORRY. WE'LL ALWAYS HAVE EACH OTHER...
MELL LAZARUS. 6-30
© FIELD ENTERPRISES, INC., 1977

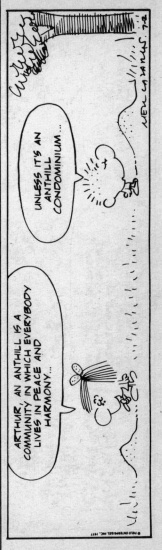

MISS PEACH

ARTHUR EXPLAINS The LAWS of NATURE →
ARTHUR, HOW COME PEOPLE ONLY HAVE BABY PEOPLE, BIRDS ONLY HAVE BABY BIRDS, CATS ONLY HAVE BABY CATS, AND SO ON ?
THE INTERNATIONAL COPYRIGHT CONVENTION OF 1913.
MEL CAZARUS.

ARTHUR EXPLAINS The LAWS of NATURE →
HOW COME WHEN I LOOK AROUND ME, I SEE ONLY THINGS THAT ARE ANIMAL, VEGETABLE OR MINERAL?
BECAUSE ALL THE OTHER STUFF IS ON THE GROCERY SHELVES.
MEL CAZARUS.

MISS PEACH

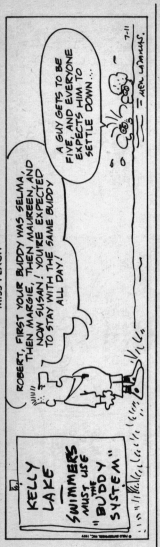

MISS PEACH

KAMP KELLY LAKE
TOMMY'S AFRAID TO COME INTO THE WATER. I GUESS HE'S TOO YOUNG!
TOMMY IS A BABY!!
I AM NOT A BABY...
IT'S JUST THAT WHO NEEDS A RUSTY DIAPER PIN..?
7-13
MELL LAZARUS
© FIELD ENTERPRISES, INC., 1977

ARTHUR EXPLAINS The LAWS of NATURE
ARTHUR, WILL THE INSECTS EVER REALLY TAKE OVER?
SURE, IF THERE'S A FREE ELECTION.
MELL LAZARUS 7-14
© FIELD ENTERPRISES, INC., 1977

MISS PEACH

ARTHUR EXPLAINS THE SOLAR SYSTEM
HOW COME THERE'S NO LIFE ON THE MOON?
FIRST OF ALL, THERE'S NOTHING MUCH TO DO THERE...
MELL LAZARUS. 7-15
© FIELD ENTERPRISES, INC., 1977

WALTER! YOU WERE TOLD NEVER TO SWIM WITHOUT A BUDDY!!
I AM, I AM!! MY BUDDY IS A SPECKLED TROUT!!
MELL LAZARUS. 7-16
© FIELD ENTERPRISES, INC., 1977

MISS PEACH

FUTURE LAWYERS' ADVERTISING AGENCY
ARTHUR, PROP.
NOW THAT LAWYERS CAN ADVERTISE, CAN YOU SUGGEST SOME COMMERCIAL THEME SONGS?
HOW ABOUT: "I'VE GOT A FEELING YOU'RE FILING," "THESE FOOLISH THINGS REMIND ME TO SUE," "TASTE OF MONEY" (FOR NEW LAWYERS WITH THEIR FIRST CASES) AND "NOLO CONTENDERE CHA CHA CHA."
© FIELD ENTERPRISES, INC., 1977
MELL LAZARUS. 7-18

ARTHUR REVEALS NATURE'S SECRETS
TELL ME ONE OF NATURE'S SECRETS, ARTHUR..!
OKAY. THAT FROG HAS MONEY IN A SWISS BANK....
© FIELD ENTERPRISES, INC., 1977
MELL LAZARUS. 7-19

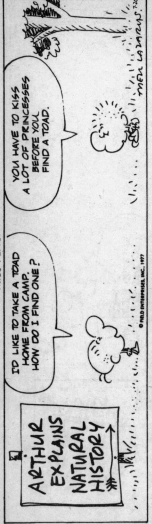

MISS PEACH

ARTHUR EXPLAINS THE LAWS OF NATURE
IS IT TRUE THAT CAMELS ONLY TAKE ONE DRINK IN SEVEN DAYS ?
ONLY THOSE CAMELS WHO ARE TRYING TO GO ON THE WAGON ...
7-27
MELL LAZARUS

ARTHUR EXPLAINS THE LAWS OF NATURE
WHERE DO THE BEES DRINK WHEN THE FLOWERS CLOSE UP AT NIGHT ?
I GUESS AT AN AFTER-FLOWERS CLUB ...
MELL LAZARUS,
7-28

ARTHUR EXPLAINS THE LAWS OF NATURE→
ARTHUR, WHY DOES THE SUN SPEND THE MORNING IN THE EAST, AND THE EVENING IN THE WEST?
BECAUSE THE WEST STAYS LIGHT LONGER...
© FIELD ENTERPRISES, INC., 1977
MELL LAZARUS. 7-29

IRA, YOU TAKE LIFE TOO SERIOUSLY. WHY CAN'T YOU LEARN TO LAUGH AT YOURSELF?
CAMP PSYCHOLOGIST
I DO, I DO, BUT MY LAUGHTER GETS DROWNED OUT BY EVERYONE ELSE'S...
© FIELD ENTERPRISES, INC., 1977
MELL LAZARUS. 7-30

Bless Our Dispensary
I HAVE A SLIGHT COLD.
TAKE AN ASPIRIN. YOU'LL BE FINE IN THE MORNING.
BY THE WAY, YOU HAVE A GOOD RECORD...DO YOU REALIZE YOU'VE NEVER BEEN SICK BEFORE – AND THIS IS YOUR 34TH DAY AT CAMP...?
Dear Folks: Today I got sick. And guess what? The nurse pointed out that my days are numbered. Love, Arthur.
MELL LAZARUS
8-1
© FIELD ENTERPRISES, INC., 1977

CAMP PSYCHOLOGIST
IRA, THE GREATEST THING IN THE WORLD IS TO LOVE AND BE LOVED!
THAT'S RIGHT, BUT I'M NOT LOVING UNTIL THEY LOVE ME FIRST!!
MELL LAZARUS
8-2
© FIELD ENTERPRISES, INC., 1977

— MISS PEACH —

MEL LAZARUS. 8-3

Panel 1: MARCIA'S SISTER USED TO GO OUT WITH A T.V. PRODUCER....!

Panel 2: YES, BUT SHE SAYS HE NEVER TOOK HER OUT FOR NICE DINNERS...

Panel 3: REALLY? WHAT FINALLY HAPPENED, MARCIA?

Panel 4: MY MOTHER CANCELLED HIM AFTER THIRTEEN HOT DOGS...

© FIELD ENTERPRISES, INC. 1977

MEL LAZARUS. 8-4

CAMP PSYCHOLOGIST

IRA, YOU MUST LEARN TO TAKE CHARGE OF YOUR OWN DESTINY. BE YOUR OWN BOSS!!

I'M NOT READY FOR A HIGH-LEVEL EXECUTIVE POSITION...

© FIELD ENTERPRISES, INC. 1977

MISS PEACH

ARTHUR EXPLAINS The LAWS of NATURE
DO ALL RABBITS MULTIPLY RAPIDLY?
ONLY THE CERTIFIED PUBLIC RABBITS...
© FIELD ENTERPRISES, INC., 1977
MELL LAZARUS. 8-5

ARTHUR, YOU DID A FINE JOB LIGHTING THE BONFIRE!
BY THE WAY, SO FAR THIS SUMMER, YOU'VE WRITTEN 40 LETTERS HOME. YOU ARE HEREBY EXCUSED FROM COMPULSORY LETTER-WRITING.
LETTERS HOME
Arthur 40
Dear Folks: ① Today I lit the bonfire. ② my writing is over for the summer. Love, Arthur
© FIELD ENTERPRISES, INC., 1977
MELL LAZARUS 8-6

IRA, WHY DO YOU SUPPOSE YOUR PARENTS HAVE GIVEN YOUR THREE-YEAR-OLD BROTHER HIS OWN PHONE, BUT NOT YOU?
IT'S AN ECONOMY MEASURE. HE HASN'T YET LEARNED TO DIAL.
CAMP PSYCHOLOGIST
MELL LAZARUS. 8-15
© FIELD ENTERPRISES, INC., 1977

IRA, YOU SAY YOU HAVE NO COURAGE? DON'T YOU THINK IT TOOK COURAGE FOR YOU TO COME TO SEE ME IN THE FIRST PLACE?
THAT'S TRUE!! A COWARD WOULD NEVER HAVE PUT ON THAT STRAITJACKET, IN FRONT OF THE WHOLE CAMP!!
CAMP PSYCHOLOGIST
8-16
MELL LAZARUS.
© FIELD ENTERPRISES, INC., 1977

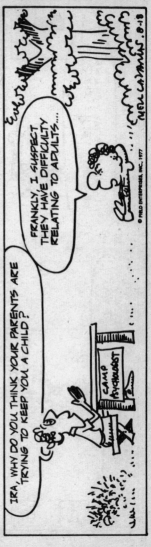

MISS PEACH

FRANCINE, YOU'RE NOT GETTING ANY YOUNGER....
I'M GOING TO PROPOSE TO YOU, AND IF YOU TURN ME DOWN, YOU MIGHT BE ALONE FOR THE REST OF YOUR LIFE. SO...
-WILL YOU MARRY ME?
FIRST, I'LL TAKE MACRAME LESSONS - THEN I'LL TAKE UP CROCHETING....
8-19
MELL LAZARUS
© FIELD ENTERPRISES, INC. 1977

IRA, DON'T YOU AGREE THAT A SUPERIORITY COMPLEX IS AS BAD AS AN INFERIORITY COMPLEX?
THAT DEPENDS ON WHETHER YOU WANT TO BE THE GROVELER OR THE GROVELEE.
MELL LAZARUS. 8-20
© FIELD ENTERPRISES, INC. 1977

MISS PEACH

IRA, YOU ARE THE SLOPPIEST CAMPER, THE WORST ATHLETE, THE MOST UNCOOPERATIVE BUNKMATE, AND A GENERAL DISAPPOINTMENT !!
CAMP DIRECTOR
YOU ARE EXCUSED.
CAMP DIRECTOR
FOR THOSE THINGS, OR JUST FROM YOUR OFFICE ?
8-22
MELL LAZARUS.
© FIELD ENTERPRISES, INC., 1977

KAMP KELLY KLARION
PRESSROOM
YOU'VE STARTED THE PRESS RUN, ARTHUR ? GOOD !!
THAT MEANS THE EDITION WILL BE OUT BY 3 O'CLOCK FOR ABSOLUTE, POSITIVE CERTAIN - RIGHT ??
EDITOR
LET'S SAY I'M ENTERTAINING THE SAME WILD HOPE ...
MELL LAZARUS. 8-23
© FIELD ENTERPRISES, INC., 1977

MISS PEACH

KAMP KELLY NATURE LORE
SKUNKS HAVE A MUCH KEENER SENSE OF SMELL THAN WE DO, ARTHUR!
Dear Folks: Today I learned that a skunk smells better than I do. Love, Arthur.
MELL LAZARUS 8-26
© FIELD ENTERPRISES, INC., 1977

KAMP KELLY KLARION
EDITORIAL OFFICES
ARTHUR, HAS THE FRONT PAGE BEEN LOCKED UP YET?
EDITOR
YES, CHIEF, BUT DON'T WORRY– WE'LL GET IT OUT OF THAT CLOSET JUST AS SOON AS THE LOCKSMITH GETS HERE ...
8-27
MELL LAZARUS.
© FIELD ENTERPRISES, INC., 1977

MISS PEACH

AH YES! I'LL NEVER FORGET— WHEN MY FATHER USED TO SAIL FOR THE AMERICA'S CUP— I WOULD SERVE ICED LEMONADE TO THE TIRED YACHTSMEN..!
Dear Folks: Today Miss Crystal told us she used to pick up sailors. Love, Arthur.
MELL LAZARUS.
8-31
© FIELD ENTERPRISES, INC., 1977

HOW ARE YOUR FIRST-AID STUDIES COMING, ARTHUR?
FINE, SIR. TODAY I TOOK DROWNING, BLEEDING AND INSECT BITES...
DISPENSARY
CLASSES TODAY
Dear Folks: Tomorrow I am Taking Poison.
MELL LAZARUS
9-1
© FIELD ENTERPRISES, INC., 1977

DOCTOR, DOES THIS MEAN I'LL HAVE TO PREPARE SPECIAL MEALS FOR ARTHUR?
NOT REALLY. HE'S ALLERGIC ONLY TO SWEETBREADS, SO JUST TAKE THEM OFF HIS PLATE....
AMP KELLY DISPEN
Dear Folks: Today the doctor ordered my Pancreas removed. Love, Arthur.
MELL LAZARUS 9-2
© FIELD ENTERPRISES, INC., 1977

HMM... I HAVEN'T GOTTEN MY FAVORITE MAGAZINE IN YEARS! I'M GOING TO COMPLAIN TO THE COMPANY....
Dear Folks: Today Mr. Grimmis came to the realization that Life is over. Love, Arthur.
MELL LAZARUS. 9-3
© FIELD ENTERPRISES, INC., 1977

MISS PEACH

IRA, ARTHUR, CAN WE LOOK FORWARD TO A NEW SCHOOL YEAR WITHOUT THE WHOLESALE CHEATING THAT USED TO GO ON?
PRINCIPAL
YES, SIR. FROM NOW ON IT WILL BE STRICTLY **RETAIL**...
IRA and ARTHUR CHEATING SERVICE
MELL LAZARUS. 9-5
© FIELD ENTERPRISES, INC. 1977

WELL, IRA, HAVE YOU LEARNED TO LAUGH AT YOURSELF, YET?
SCHOOL PSYCHOLOGIST
NO, BUT AT LEAST I DON'T **CRY** SO MUCH WHEN **OTHER** PEOPLE LAUGH AT ME...
MELL LAZARUS. 9-6
© FIELD ENTERPRISES, INC. 1977

I LIKE THE WAY YOU LOOK IN YOUR NEW EYEGLASSES, LINDA!
I DON'T.
WHY NOT?
I FEEL LIKE I'M WINDOW-SHOPPING...
MELL LAZARUS. 9-7
© FIELD ENTERPRISES, INC., 1977

IRA, HAVE YOU BEEN DILIGENTLY APPLYING THE PROGRAM I TAUGHT YOU TO COMBAT ENNUI?
SCHOOL PSYCHOLOGIST
I WAS, SIR, BUT I GOT BORED...
MELL LAZARUS. 9-8
© FIELD ENTERPRISES, INC., 1977

MISS PEACH

Panel 1: IRA, I'M GOING TO SUGGEST TO YOUR PARENTS THAT THEY GET YOU AN ENGLISH TUTOR ...

PRINCIPAL

Panel 2: IF IT'S ALL THE SAME TO YOU, I'D RATHER TRY THE FRENCH HORN...!

MELL LAZARUS 9-12

Panel 3: ARTHUR, WHAT'S THE HEADLINE ON THE STORY ABOUT MR. GRIMMIS' FAMOUS COLLECTION OF PHOTOS OF DRINKING STEINS BEING LOST AND THEN FOUND BY THE POLICE?

KELLY SCHOOL KLARION NEWS ROOM →

EDITOR

Panel 4: "POLICE TURN OVER MR. GRIMMIS' MUG SHOTS."

MELL LAZARUS 9-13

—MISS PEACH—

IRA, YOU'RE NOT BEING FAIR ABOUT YOUR PARENTS. I'VE MET THEM, AND THEY'RE PERFECTLY LOVELY PEOPLE!

HAVE YOU EVER HEARD OF DR. AND MRS. JEKYLL AND MR. AND MRS. HYDE?

SCHOOL PSYCHOLOGIST

MEL CASANUS. 9-16

ARTHUR, I'D LIKE TO STAY OUT LATER THAN MIDNIGHT ONCE IN A WHILE. HOW CAN I DO IT?

TELL YOUR PARENTS YOU'RE DATING A WEREWOLF — BUT FROM A WEALTHY FAMILY, AND WHO IS GETTING THE GRADES FOR LAW SCHOOL...

ARTHUR'S ADVICE ON FOOLPROOF WAYS TO GET AWAY WITH MURDER AT HOME.

MEL CASANUS. 9-17

MISS PEACH

IRA, YOUR CONDUCT DOES NOT WARRANT YOUR GOING TO THE ZOO WITH US TODAY. PERHAPS YOU SHOULD GO TO THE PRINCIPAL'S OFFICE, INSTEAD...
IN ITS WAY, JUST AS INTERESTING.
9-19
MEL LAZARUS.
© FIELD ENTERPRISES, INC., 1977

IRA, MISS PEACH HAS REPEATEDLY COMPLAINED, ABOUT YOUR CONDUCT. DON'T YOU THINK A CHANGE IS IN ORDER?
PRINCIPAL
YES, SIR, BUT MISS PEACH HAS TENURE...
9-20
MEL LAZARUS.
© FIELD ENTERPRISES, INC., 1977

MISS PEACH

IRA, YOU SAY YOU HAVE A WILD FANTASY INVOLVING MISS PEACH? UH, WHAT IS THAT FANTASY?
SHE GIVES ME A PASSING ENGLISH MARK...
MELL LAZARUS. 9-21
© FIELD ENTERPRISES, INC., 1977

ARTHUR ANSWERS ANY QUESTION
THE BOYS WHO LIKE ME ARE ALL NERDS, WHILE NONE OF THE TERRIFIC GUYS EVER LIKE ME, AND IF ONE EVER SAYS HE DOES, HE AUTOMATICALLY BECOMES A NERD.
DO YOU LIKE ME?
AT LAST— THE TRULY UNANSWERABLE QUESTION!!
9-22
MELL LAZARUS.
© FIELD ENTERPRISES, INC., 1977

MISS PEACH

MISS PEACH

LET MARCIA MASON GIVE YOU A PHILOSOPHY OF LIFE
YOU KNOW, MARCIA, I WOULD HATE TO BECOME JUST ONE OF THE FACELESS MILLIONS...
I CAN'T IMAGINE WHY, WITH YOUR FACE...
MELL LAZARUS.
9-28
© FIELD ENTERPRISES, INC., 1977

I DON'T KNOW WHY YOU TWO PERSIST IN COPYING FROM EACH OTHER'S TEST PAPERS. AFTER ALL, YOU'RE BOTH SO DUMB...!
PRINCIPAL
WELL ?? WHO ELSE WOULD ALLOW COPYING FOR FREE?
MELL LAZARUS.
9-29
© FIELD ENTERPRISES, INC., 1977

MISS PEACH

IRA, DO YOU STILL HAVE MEMORIES OF WHEN YOU WERE SMALL?
I DON'T REMEMBER EVER FEELING SMALL.
HOWEVER, I DO REMEMBER THINGS BEING BIG..
SCHOOL PSYCHOLOGIST
10-3
MELL LAZARUS.

ARTHUR'S PROBLEM CLINIC FOR KIDS WITH PROBLEMS WITH PARENTS
MY MOTHER AND FATHER TELL ME I NEED THEIR APPROVAL TO GO OUT ON DATES. IS THIS FAIR?
SURE. THAT'S WHAT IS MEANT BY "TWO CONSENTING ADULTS..."
MELL LAZARUS. 10.4

MISS PEACH

KELLY SCHOOL Friends of The BIRDS MEET HERE
BUT IF YOU GO SOUTH FOR THE WINTER, YOU WILL LEAVE OUR AIR DEVOID OF SONG...!
WHAT DOES HE WANT US TO DO, CHIP IN AND BUY HIM A PORTABLE RADIO?
MELL LAZARUS.
10-7

MISS CRYSTAL WILL TALK ABOUT THE ORIGINS OF WORDS!
I SUPPOSE YOU'RE WONDERING WHAT QUALIFIES ME TO SPEAK ON THE SUBJECT OF WORDS..
NO, WE'RE NOT... AFTER ALL, YOU'VE BEEN USING THEM LONGER THAN ANYONE IN THE SCHOOL...
10-8
MELL LAZARUS.

MISS PEACH

IRA, BEFORE ONE CAN FEEL BRAVE, ONE MUST FIRST BE AFRAID!
SCHOOL PSYCHOLOGIST
WITH ME IT WAS THE OPPOSITE — FIRST I FELT BRAVE, THEN I GOT PUNCHED IN THE MOUTH...
MELL LAZARUS. 10-17
© FIELD ENTERPRISES, INC., 1977

FRANCINE, I'M SITTING HERE THINKING ABOUT THE LOVE OF MY LIFE, MY GUIDING LIGHT, MY SWEETHEART, MY INSPIRATION. I'M THINKING OF YOU.
CALL ME WHEN YOU START THINKING OF ME BEFORE ALL THOSE OTHER GIRLS...
MELL LAZARUS. 10-18
© FIELD ENTERPRISES, INC., 1977

MISS PEACH

IRA, A STUDENT WHO CAN'T HANDLE THE WORKLOAD USUALLY GETS THROWN OUT OF SCHOOL!
PRINCIPAL
GEE - ISN'T IT WONDERFUL HOW NATURE COMPENSATES?!
MELL LAZARUS. 10·19

KELLY SCHOOL SWEETHEART SERVICE
LET US FILL YOUR SOCIAL NEEDS
I WANT TWO BOYFRIENDS -- NO. 1 FOR MEETING ALL MY INTELLECTUAL NEEDS, AND NO. 2 JUST FOR SILLY FUN STUFF!
OKAY. WOULD YOU MIND IF NO. 1 HAD A GIRL ON THE SIDE TO TAKE UP THE SLACK?
MELL LAZARUS. 10-20

IRA, TAKE MY WORD FOR IT— YOUR PARENTS LOVE YOU !!
SCHOOL PSYCHOLOGIST
YOU MEAN YOU'VE SPOKEN TO THEM SINCE I LEFT HOME THIS MORNING ?
MELL LAZARUS.
10-21
© FIELD ENTERPRISES, INC., 1977

The Kelly School PROBLEM CLINIC for GIRLS with PROBLEMS with BOYS
MY BOYFRIEND FLIRTS SHAMELESSLY! WHAT SHOULD I DO??
AS LONG AS IT'S WITH YOU, NOTHING..!
10-22
MELL LAZARUS.

MISS PEACH

MARCIA'S ADVICE ON HUMAN RELATIONS
HOW CAN I TELL IF IRA LIES TO ME?
DO YOU ASK HIM QUESTIONS?
WHY, YES...
HE LIES TO YOU.
10-28
MELL LAZARUS.
© FIELD ENTERPRISES, INC. 1977

marcia's ADVICE ON HUMAN RELATIONS
PEOPLE ALWAYS TELL ME TO GET LOST. WHAT'S WRONG WITH ME?
AMONG OTHER THINGS, YOU NEVER LISTEN.
MELL LAZARUS.
10-29
© FIELD ENTERPRISES, INC. 1977

MISS PEACH

ARTHUR HAS ALL THE ANSWERS TO YOUR SCIENCE QUESTIONS!
HOW DID THE WORLD COME TO BE?
WELL, ONE DAY, A PIECE FLEW OFF THE SUN, SEE, AND FLEW AROUND IN SPACE FOR A WHILE, UNTIL ONE AFTERNOON, A DESIGNER AT DISNEYLAND...
MELL LAZARUS.
10-31
© FIELD ENTERPRISES, INC., 1977

LET ARTHUR CHANGE YOUR BAD NEWS TO GOOD NEWS!
I SPENT MY ALLOWANCE, AND WILL BE BROKE FOR THE REST OF THE WEEK!
HOW LUCKY!! YOU'LL NEVER AGAIN HAVE TO WORRY ABOUT INFLATION UNTIL FRIDAY..!
11-1
MELL LAZARUS.
© FIELD ENTERPRISES, INC., 1977

MISS PEACH

ARTHUR
CAN CHANGE
your
BAD NEWS
TO
GOOD NEWS
→

I BOUGHT AN ICE CREAM CONE, AND BEFORE I HAD EVEN TASTED IT, IT FELL TO THE GROUND...

WHAT A CLEVER HOSTESS! FOR WHAT— MAYBE 25 CENTS— YOU THREW A PARTY FOR 350,000 ANTS!

MELL LAZARUS. 11-2

© FIELD ENTERPRISES, INC. 1977

ARTHUR, YOUR GRADES ARE TERRIBLE! DON'T YOU REALIZE NOBODY WANTS A DOPE ON THEIR PAYROLL?

PRINCIPAL

YES, I DO. I INTEND TO FREE-LANCE.

MELL LAZARUS. 11-3

© FIELD ENTERPRISES, INC. 1977

MISS PEACH

GROUP Therapy TODAY
WHICH OF YOU WOULD LIKE TO TELL US HIS WORST FEARS?
NOT ME. I'M SCARED OF PUBLIC SPEAKING....
© FIELD ENTERPRISES, INC., 1977
MEL LAZARUS
11-14

GROUP Therapy TODAY.
ONE MAY SPEAK FREELY HERE, SO LESTER WILL TELL US WHAT HE HONESTLY THINKS OF IRA.
BEFORE HE DOES, A QUESTION: MAY WE ALSO **HIT** FREELY?
© FIELD ENTERPRISES, INC., 1977
MEL LAZARUS
11-15

MISS PEACH

ARTHUR FINALLY ANSWERS THE ETERNAL QUESTIONS
TELL ME, ARTHUR, WHY ARE WE HERE?
BECAUSE THEY DON'T WANT US THERE.
11-21
MELL LAZARUS.

ARTHUR FINALLY ANSWERS THE ETERNAL QUESTIONS
ARTHUR, DOES THE UNIVERSE HAVE A GRAND DESIGN?
NO. IT'S GOOD, BUT NOT GRAND.
11-22
MELL LAZARUS.

ARTHUR FINALLY ANSWERS THE ETERNAL QUESTIONS
WHERE DO WE HUMAN BEINGS FIT IN THE GREATER SCHEME OF THINGS?
YOU FIT IN THE 3RD ROW, 2ND SEAT, AND I FIT IN THE 5TH ROW, 4TH SEAT.
MEL LAZARUS
11-23

ARTHUR FINALLY ANSWERS THE ETERNAL QUESTIONS
HOW DID ADAM AND EVE GET HERE?
BY BUS. THEY WERE AFRAID THEY WOULDN'T FIND A PARKING SPACE.
MEL LAZARUS
11-24

ARTHUR FINALLY ANSWERS THE ETERNAL QUESTIONS
© FIELD ENTERPRISES, INC., 1977
ARTHUR, CAN YOU TELL ME WHEN THE WORLD WILL COME TO AN END?
CERTAINLY. IT WILL OCCUR SOME-TIME BETWEEN 2:45 TODAY, WHEN MR. GRIMMIS SEES YOUR MIDTERM MARKS, AND TOMORROW AT 9:AM, WHEN YOUR FATHER COMES TO SCHOOL...
MEL LAZARUS
11-25

ARTHUR ANSWERS, FINALLY, THE ETERNAL QUESTIONS
© FIELD ENTERPRISES, INC., 1977
ARTHUR, IS THERE ANY LIFE AFTER DEATH?
SOMETIMES, ON SATURDAY NIGHTS.
MEL LAZARUS.
11-26

MISS PEACH

MISS PEACH

MISS PEACH

ARTHUR STRIMM
EXPERT ON INTERNATIONAL AFFAIRS.
ARTHUR, TELL ME ABOUT INTERNATIONAL AFFAIRS.
OF COURSE. THEY USUALLY START WITH A RENDEZVOUS IN A SMALL CAFE, SOFT MUSIC, AND A BOTTLE OF WINE, VINO OR VIN, DEPENDING ON WHERE...
12-7
MELL LAZARUS.

IRA, WHY AREN'T YOU DOING A SCIENCE EXPERIMENT?
I AM, MR. GRIMMIS. IT'S CALLED, "THE EFFECTS ON THE HUMAN BODY OF PROLONGED INERTIA."
12-8
MELL LAZARUS.

PARENTS USUALLY EXPECT THEIR CHILDREN TO GO FARTHER, ACADEMICALLY, THAN THEY THEMSELVES DID!
RIGHT, MISS PEACH! MY FATHER HAS A DEGREE IN PHILOSOPHY. HE WANTS ME TO STRIVE TO BECOME A DISC JOCKEY...
MELL LAZARUS.
12-9

ARTHUR'S ADVICE ON HOW TO KEEP FROM GETTING INVOLVED
SOME BOY WANTS TO GIVE ME AN ENGAGEMENT RING. IT'S A BEAUTIFUL, EXPENSIVE RING.... BUT I DON'T WANT TO ENCOURAGE HIM...
NO PROBLEM. ACCEPT THE RING, AND HOCK IT.
MELL LAZARUS.
12-10

MISS PEACH

ARTHUR ANSWERS YOUR QUESTIONS ABOUT SOCIAL STRATA and CASTE SYSTEMS
MY QUESTION IS, SHOULD A PERSON ON MY VERY HIGH SOCIO-ECONOMIC LEVEL BE SEEKING ADVICE FROM A JERK LIKE YOU?
MEL LAZARUS. 12·14

ARTHUR ANSWERS QUESTIONS ABOUT SOCIAL STRATA and CASTE SYSTEMS
I'M ON SUCH A HIGH LEVEL THAT I HAVE NOBODY TO RELATE TO. WHAT SHOULD I DO?
SWALLOW YOUR PRIDE AND CALL THE PRESIDENT OF THE UNITED STATES....
MEL LAZARUS.

MISS PEACH

I NEVER WEAR A MUFFLER OR HAT, WHATEVER THE WEATHER!
THAT'S AN INCREDIBLY STUPID ATTITUDE...!
YOU'RE RIGHT. I GOT A REALLY BAD COLD IN MY HEAD.
AT LEAST THAT'S SOMETHING...
12-19
MELL LAZARUS.

ARTHUR'S GIFT ADVICE
WHAT SHOULD I GIVE THE MAN WHO HAS EVERYTHING?
A COPY OF MY NEW BOOK, "SHARE AND SHARE ALIKE."
12-20
MELL LAZARUS.

ABOUT THE AUTHOR

Mell Lazarus is the cartoonist/ writer of the comic strip MOMMA which appears in over 200 newspapers in the United States. In addition to creating MOMMA, which won the National Cartoonists Society award, Lazarus is the man behind MISS PEACH and the author of three plays and a novel. When asked how his own mother feels about the comic strip characterization, Lazarus replied, "She says it's very funny, but she doesn't identify with it. She thinks I'm doing my Aunt Helen."